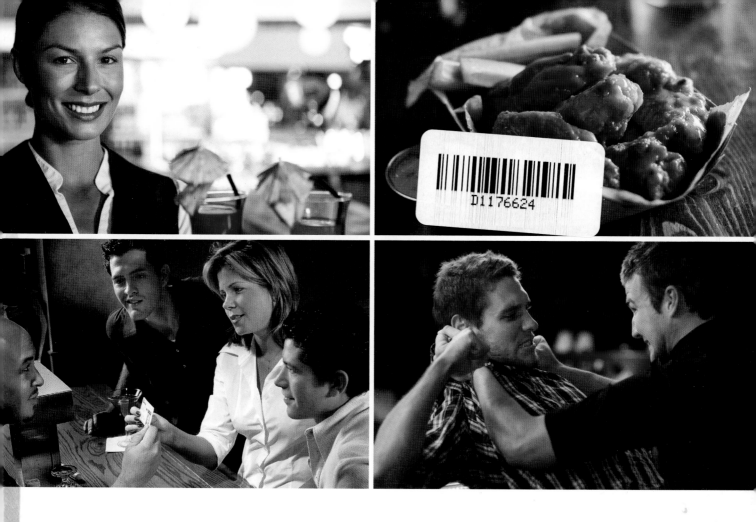

3ʳᵈ EDITION

SERVSAFE®
ALCOHOL GUIDE

ServSafe
National Restaurant Association

DISCLAIMER

TABLE OF CONTENTS

CHAPTER 3: Checking Identification

CHAPTER 4: Handling Difficult Situations

Answer Key and Index

ACKNOWLEDGMENTS

The development of the *ServSafe Alcohol® Guide, Third Edition* would not have been possible without the expertise of our many advisors and reviewers. Thank you to the following people and organizations for their time, effort, and dedication to creating this third edition.

Cindy Brison, Nebraska Extension

Michael J. Camire, New England Food Service Consulting

Dimitrios G. Christopoulos, Christopoulos Law Group, LLC

Deet Gilbert, Johnson and Wales University

Trista Kimber, Hooters of America

Victor J. Martinez, New Mexico Restaurant Association

Terrence Pappas, Monical Pizza Corporation

Keith Parish, Ivy Tech Community College

Kevin Settles, Bardenay Restaurants & Distilleries

Donald Vita, Hoosier Hospitality Consulting

A MESSAGE FROM
THE NATIONAL RESTAURANT ASSOCIATION

The National Restaurant Association is pleased to bring you the *ServSafe Alcohol® Guide, Third Edition.*

Risk management is crucial to the success of every restaurant and foodservice operation and bar establishment. Serving alcohol responsibly is critical for protecting your customers, your community, and your business. To develop these materials, we convened foodservice, regulatory, legal, academic, medical, and insurance experts to build a training program that focuses on what front-of-the-house employees need to know to serve alcohol responsibly.

By opening this guide, you have made a significant commitment to responsible alcohol service. ServSafe Alcohol is designed to train all members of an establishment, including servers, bartenders, hosts, valets, bouncers, coat checkers, or anyone who interacts with guests who consume alcohol. The program covers alcohol law and your responsibility, recognizing and preventing intoxication, checking identification, and handling difficult situations.

We applaud you for making the commitment to serving alcohol responsibly. Your training is a beneficial step toward making your operation and your community safe. For more information on ServSafe Alcohol, please visit ServSafe.com/ServSafe-Alcohol.

CHAPTER 1

Alcohol Law and Your Responsibility

What do you like about serving alcohol?

"Why serve drinks? Because I like the people, and it gets them to open up. I like getting to know everyone and hearing about what's happening around town."

"You're probably going to think I'm crazy, but I really like serving when it's busy. I love the rush that comes with working hard to get guests their drinks quickly. Plus, make people happy on a busy night and you're going to get some great tips!"

"Being a mixologist is fun! I like when people ask for recommendations. And then when they take that first sip and I can tell they like it—I made them feel that way!"

OBJECTIVES

After completing this chapter, you will be able to identify the following:

- Costs of not serving alcohol responsibly
- Three types of liability related to alcohol service
- Laws for alcohol service

Serving alcohol can let you show off a skill and help people have fun while you have fun, too! And you can make a nice living. But before you get to do those things, you need to understand alcohol service laws and your responsibility.

In this first chapter, you'll learn some of the basics that everyone serving alcohol needs to know. This includes the costs of not serving alcohol responsibly, your responsibilities when serving alcohol, and the laws that affect you when doing it.

COSTS OF NOT SERVING ALCOHOL RESPONSIBLY

No one likes to think about the costs of not serving alcohol responsibly. But if you want to serve alcohol, you should also know the costs of irresponsible service. These can include the following.

Human costs. Serving alcohol irresponsibly sometimes leads to people getting hurt. In serious cases, those injuries can last a lifetime. Some people even die.

Legal costs. There are legal consequences for the business, too. Owners, managers, and employees may face:

- Fines
- Lawsuits
- Criminal charges

Business costs. Irresponsible service can hurt profits:

- Loss of liquor license—The liquor license can be temporarily suspended. It can even be permanently revoked.

- Loss of revenue—The bad publicity after an incident can cause a loss in customers. That means a big loss of revenue, which means jobs might be cut.

- Increased insurance costs or loss of insurance—The establishment will have to pay more for insurance premiums. It may not be able to get insured at all.

What does "being liable" mean? →

Hurting others, losing a job, and getting your bosses into legal trouble are all bad. But what about you? Did you know that you can be held personally liable if you break liquor laws? Being liable means you are legally responsible for something. In other words, if you serve irresponsibly, you might find yourself facing legal consequences, too.

TYPES OF LIABILITY

When selling or serving alcohol, you are liable, or legally responsible, for your actions. This means both the things you do and the things you do not do. Three types of liability apply to you:

- Criminal liability
- Civil liability, including dram shop laws
- Administrative liability

Criminal Liability

States, counties, cities, and towns write laws about how alcohol is supposed to be served. You are responsible for making sure you do not break these alcohol laws. If you do, you can be held responsible for committing a crime. This is criminal liability. For example, most states will hold you criminally liable if you serve alcohol to someone who is underage or intoxicated.

Can you go to jail for breaking alcohol laws? →

Criminal liability can result in:

- Jail time
- Probation
- Fines

Civil Liability

Civil liability focuses on compensating people who were hurt by someone who was negligent. For alcohol service, this means someone who did not serve responsibly. Translation? Lawsuits.

If you break alcohol laws and somebody gets hurt, you can be sued and forced to pay damages. This can happen if you contributed to a person's injury or if you did not prevent someone from getting hurt.

Dram Shop Laws

Many states also have dram shop laws. They are a special kind of civil liability for people who sell alcohol. Dram shop laws allow a person who was not even at a business to sue for injuries caused by a guest who was drinking there.

Who could be sued if an intoxicated driver kills someone on the way home? →

For example, say someone has several drinks at your establishment and leaves intoxicated. On the drive home, your guest kills another driver. Under dram shop laws, the business, the owner, the manager, and the employees can be sued for the death of the other driver.

Administrative Liability

Administrative liability deals with penalties for establishments and employees who do not follow alcohol laws. These penalties are given by agencies called liquor authorities. Each state and many municipalities have one.

Liquor authorities:

- Grant liquor licenses
- Help enforce state and local liquor laws
- Can penalize establishments and employees who break alcohol laws

Penalties from liquor authorities can include, but are not limited to:

- Suspension or loss of the establishment's liquor license
- Loss of a server's right to serve alcohol
- Fines against owners and staff

APPLY YOUR KNOWLEDGE

Types of Liability

Directions: For each situation, identify which type of liability applies. Some types of liability may be used more than once.

Situation		Liability
1.	_C_ An establishment's liquor license was revoked for serving intoxicated guests.	A. Civil liability
2.	_A_ A pedestrian who was hit by a drunk driver sues the restaurant that served the driver.	B. Criminal liability
3.	_B_ A server is sentenced to 60 days of probation for serving alcohol to an underage guest.	C. Administrative liability
4.	_A_ An intoxicated guest is injured in a fall and sues the establishment that served him.	

For answers, see page 1-12.

LAWS RESTRICTING ALCOHOL SERVICE

Each state has its own set of liquor laws. So do many counties, cities, and towns. And their laws are usually stricter than the state laws. To keep your guests safe, learn the laws that apply to you and how they work.

Laws to Prevent Underage Drinking

All states have laws designed to keep underage people from drinking alcohol. Here are some of the more common ones.

Minimum age to buy, possess, or drink alcohol. In most states, it is illegal for people under 21 to:

- Try to buy alcohol
- Possess alcohol
- Drink alcohol regardless of how they get it

Sale and supply to underage people. In most states, it is illegal to sell or give alcohol to someone who is younger than 21.

What should you do if you see someone pass a drink to an underage guest? →

- This law applies regardless of who provides the alcohol—your establishment, the employees, or even your guests. If you see people pass drinks to an underage guest, the best practice is to stop service and remove any alcohol. There may also be other steps to take depending on the law and your company policy.
- Keep in mind that in some states, parents or legal guardians can serve alcohol to their underage children.

Use of fake or altered IDs. It is illegal for underage people to use fake or altered IDs to purchase alcohol. This means that when you are serving alcohol, you have to carefully check IDs to make sure they are genuine.

Minimum age to enter a bar. In some areas, underage people are not allowed to enter a bar. Some establishments take this a step further by requiring guests be even older than 21 just to enter the bar area. For example, an establishment might set a minimum age of 30 to enter the bar area.

Minimum age for servers and bartenders. In some states, the minimum age for servers and bartenders is 21. In many other states, servers can be younger than 21.

NOTICE
YOU MUST BE AT LEAST 21 TO ENTER THIS AREA.

IN THE NEWS

What are the consequences of serving an intoxicated guest? Here is a true story about what happened when a guest was served too much at one establishment.

A 26-year-old woman spent the day drinking with a friend at a popular beach-side bar. By late afternoon, she was visibly intoxicated.

While her friend was distracted settling the bill, the woman went by herself to the unattended valet lot. There, she took a car that wasn't hers!

Sadly, she crashed the stolen car head-on into another vehicle, killing herself and severely injuring the other driver.

The injured driver was forced to undergo numerous surgeries. Eventually, she had to move into an assisted living facility.

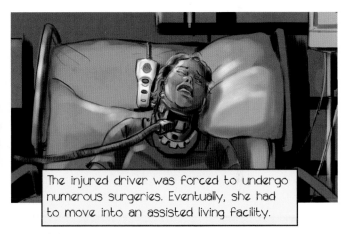

The bar later paid a 1.5-million-dollar settlement to the victim to compensate her for her injuries.

The bar was also forced to pay fines to the liquor authority. Its liquor license was also revoked because employees had acted irresponsibly in a similar situation.

Laws on Serving Intoxicated Guests

Most states also have laws designed to prevent intoxicated people from drinking even more alcohol.

Selling and serving alcohol to intoxicated guests. When an intoxicated person keeps drinking, tragedy can result.

Can a guest be held liable for passing drinks to an intoxicated person? →

- Most states have laws against selling alcohol to people who are visibly or obviously intoxicated. Some of these laws specifically hold the establishment and servers liable.
- Most laws state that any person may be held liable for serving an intoxicated person. In other words, if a guest passes drinks to someone who is intoxicated, that guest can face legal action.

Serving known alcoholics. Some states hold the establishment and its employees liable for serving a person who is known to be an alcoholic.

Other Common Laws on Alcohol Service

What are the laws on alcohol service? →

There are other alcohol service laws that are common in many states.

Try the following questions to see if you already know some of these laws. Write your answers in the space provided. After checking the answers, keep reading to learn why they are correct.

	Question	Choices
1. __C__	Can you drink alcohol on the job?	A. Yes
2. __B̶ C__	Can guests bring alcohol onto the premises?	B. No
3. __B__	Can people continue drinking past the hours of service listed on an establishment's liquor license?	C. It depends

Answers: 1 C, 2 C, 3 B

Drinking alcohol on the job. Lots of areas have laws against drinking on the job. Even if it is not specifically illegal in your area, your company probably has a policy against it. This is because drinking can impair judgment. If you drink on the job:

- You will have a harder time knowing when your guests have had enough.
- You can make other bad decisions. These can cost you and your establishment.

Bringing alcohol onto the premises. It is illegal for guests to bring their own alcohol onto the premises unless this is permitted by law and your company policy.

Following the hours of service. The legal hours for the sale and service of alcohol are listed on the establishment's liquor license. These hours apply to both guests and employees. The hours must be strictly followed.

Illegal Activities on the Premises

Establishments and employees who knowingly permit certain illegal activities can be held liable.

Gambling and Prostitution. In most states, you can be liable if you knowingly permit illegal activities such as gambling, prostitution, and other lewd behavior.

Drinking Games and Contests. In many states, it is illegal to let people play games that involve drinking alcohol. This includes popular games like beer pong and quarters. These types of games encourage people to drink to intoxication.

Illegal Drugs. You cannot knowingly permit people to possess, sell, or use illegal drugs on the premises.

Discrimination Against Guests

States also hold the owners and operators of establishments and their employees liable if they discriminate against guests due to:

- Race
- Color
- Gender
- Sexual orientation
- Age
- Disability
- Religion or creed

Want to avoid problems? Treat everyone the same!

This includes pregnant women. Refusing to serve alcohol to a woman because she is pregnant is gender discrimination.

Can you refuse alcohol service to a woman because she's pregnant?
→

SELF-CHECK

Directions: Read the question and choose the best answer.

1. **A guest may bring alcohol onto the premises when the**
   A. guest pays a corkage fee.
   B. law and company policy allow it.
   C. establishment's liquor license is temporarily suspended.
   D. guest agrees to not sue the establishment in case of injury.

2. **A guest appears to be intoxicated but wants another drink. What is the correct thing to do?**
   A. Serve a weaker drink.
   B. Serve food with the drink.
   C. Do not serve the guest alcohol.
   D. Do not serve the guest anything.

3. **Which is a penalty associated with criminal liability?**
   A. Time in prison
   B. Loss of liquor license
   C. Loss of a server permit
   D. Lawsuits from injured parties

4. **Which is an example of administrative liability?**
   A. A manager fires an employee due to serving an intoxicated guest.
   B. The police arrest an establishment owner for allowing gambling.
   C. A couple sues an establishment for serving a guest who injured them.
   D. The liquor authority revokes a license for serving underage guests.

5. **Which is a responsibility of a liquor authority?**
   A. Ensure no underage guests try to drink alcohol.
   B. Monitor establishments for compliance with liquor laws.
   C. File lawsuits on behalf of injured guests seeking compensation.
   D. Arrest establishment owners and employees for criminal violations.

6. **In most states, it is illegal to serve alcohol to guests who are**
   A. disabled.
   B. pregnant.
   C. under 21 years of age.
   D. addicted to gambling or drugs.

For answers, see page 1-12.

Answer Key

Apply Your Knowledge: Types of Liability

1. C

2. A

3. B

4. A

Self-Check

1. B

2. C

3. A

4. D

5. B

6. C

Notes

CHAPTER 2

Recognizing and Preventing Intoxication

How do you know when a guest is becoming intoxicated?

"Sometimes it's obvious that someone's had too much. People slur or stumble around. But a guest can also be over the limit and not look like it. That's a harder call, and it makes me nervous."

"Work can be crazy, but I always make a point of noticing how someone acts when they first come in. Then I watch if their behavior changes. I also watch for people who might be at risk of getting intoxicated, like inexperienced drinkers or someone who's in a bad mood."

"I think I've gotten pretty good at telling who's feeling the effects. It's easier to tell if you talk with people and know what to look for. Plus, I count the drinks I serve them."

OBJECTIVES

After completing this chapter, you will be able to identify the following:

- What alcohol is
- How alcohol moves through the body
- Factors that affect BAC
- How to assess guests
- How to count drinks
- How to estimate BAC
- Signs of intoxication
- How to prevent intoxication

This chapter deals with biology—specifically, how alcohol affects your body. That's because learning a little biology can go a long way toward helping you prevent intoxication and keep people safe.

In this chapter, you'll learn what alcohol is, how it moves through the body, and why certain factors can affect a person's level of intoxication. You'll also learn how to assess a guest's level of intoxication and ways to keep your guests from becoming intoxicated in the first place.

WHAT ALCOHOL IS

There are different kinds of alcohol. The kind we drink is called beverage alcohol, or ethanol. Beverage alcohol is typically made through two processes.

Fermentation. Some types of alcohol are made by fermenting plants, such as berries and fruits, or grains such as barley. During fermentation, yeast breaks down these plants and grains. This is what produces ethanol. Both beer and wine are created through the fermentation process.

Distillation. Other types of alcohol are made by first fermenting plants or grains and then distilling them. Distillation removes water from the alcohol. This makes the drink stronger. Spirits like vodka and whiskey are made this way.

Measuring the Strength of Alcohol

Regardless of how it is made, it is important to know the strength of different types of alcohol. This is important so you can properly count drinks and assess people's levels of intoxication.

Do you already know how the strength of alcohol is measured? See if you can rank these bottles of liquor from weakest to strongest. Use "1" for the weakest and "4" for the strongest. After checking the answers, keep reading to learn why they are correct.

Which is stronger? →

A. _____   B. _____   C. _____   D. _____

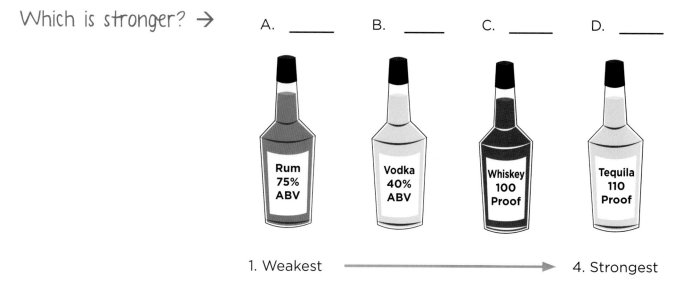

1. Weakest ————————————→ 4. Strongest

Answers: A.4, B.1, C.2, D.3

Proof

Historically, alcohol manufacturers have used the term "proof" to indicate the strength of liquor. By dividing the proof by two, you can determine how much alcohol a liquor contains.

$$\text{Strength of liquor} = \frac{\text{Proof}}{2}$$

Here are a couple of examples using the formula.

Example 1. A 100-proof whiskey is 50% alcohol because 100 divided by 2 equals 50.

Example 2. An 80-proof vodka is 40% alcohol because 80 divided by 2 equals 40.

ABV (Alcohol by Volume)

Most manufacturers indicate the strength of liquor by listing its Alcohol By Volume (ABV). The ABV is the percentage of a drink that is alcohol. For example, if a bottle of vodka has an ABV of 40%, that means that 40% of the liquid in the bottle is alcohol.

Typical Strength of Liquors

Alcoholic beverages vary in strength.

Distilled spirits. These typically range from an ABV of 20% for liqueurs, like schnapps, to 40% or higher for spirits such as vodka, whiskey, and rum.

Wine. In the U.S., wine typically has an ABV between 12 and 14%. Be aware that some types of wine contain distilled spirits. These may have an ABV that is higher than the average.

What is the typical strength of beer in the U.S.? →

Beer. The typical ABV for beer is 4% to 6%. But many craft beers today range from 2.5% to 15% ABV.

ALCOHOL'S PATH THROUGH THE BODY

For the most part, alcohol moves through a person's body in a similar manner to food. But unlike food, alcohol does not need to be digested to reach the bloodstream.

How Alcohol Gets into the Bloodstream

Here is what happens when a person drinks alcohol.

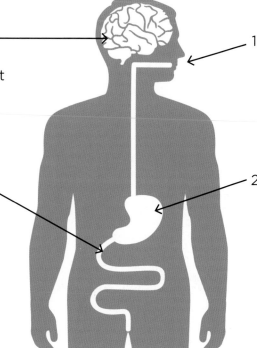

4. **Brain.** Once in the bloodstream, alcohol travels quickly throughout the body. It reaches the brain in minutes.

3. **Small Intestine.** From the stomach, the alcohol moves into the small intestine. Most of the alcohol is absorbed into the bloodstream from here.

1. **Mouth.** A small amount of alcohol is immediately absorbed from the mouth into the bloodstream.

2. **Stomach.** The rest of the alcohol moves into the stomach. Some is absorbed into the bloodstream through the stomach wall.

Because alcohol is a depressant, it slows or reduces brain activity. As people drink, areas of the brain become affected. Areas of the brain affecting these processes are especially impacted:

- Major motor skills
- Coordination
- Memory
- Judgment

How much alcohol can be in the bloodstream before the brain is affected? →

Once alcohol affects these areas of the brain, they do not work as well as they normally would. This effect can make a number of tasks dangerous, including driving.

What Blood Alcohol Content (BAC) Is

BAC stands for Blood Alcohol Content. You might also hear it called Blood Alcohol Concentration. BAC is the amount of alcohol in a person's bloodstream. You have probably heard people talk about BAC as a percentage, such as .08 or .10. This is the percentage of a person's blood that is alcohol.

Legal limit for driving. Research has shown that a person's motor skills can be significantly affected at .08. As a result, all 50 states (as of 2017) have defined the legal level of intoxication for driving at .08. Keep in mind that people can be impaired at lower BAC levels.

Quantity of alcohol affecting the brain. It doesn't take much alcohol in the bloodstream before the brain becomes affected. Just a teaspoonful of alcohol in the bloodstream of a 150-pound man can raise his BAC to .08. (This is pure alcohol or ethanol.)

Risks of Excessive Consumption

If a person's motor skills can be significantly affected at .08, what about BACs that are higher than that? Things get worse. In fact, if someone has a BAC of .30 or higher, it can lead to a coma or even death. That's why binge drinking— or drinking large amounts of alcohol in a short amount of time—is so very dangerous.

IN THE NEWS

Every year, binge drinking claims a lot of lives. Here is just one story that illustrates this. But keep in mind, binge drinking is not limited to just young people.

It was Mark's 21st birthday. He was excited, but his friends were chomping at the bit. He could finally drink with them.

As a rite of passage, they insisted on taking him out to a local tavern to complete the "21 for 21" challenge. It's where someone turning 21 attempts to drink 21 shots of alcohol—one for each birthday.

Mark never completed the challenge. Sometime after his twelfth shot, his friends brought him home.

At about 4:00 a.m., family members found him unresponsive and took him to the hospital.

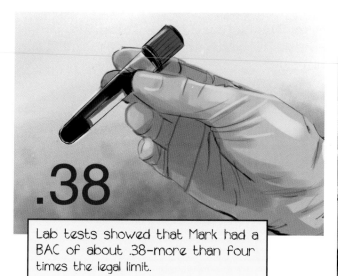

.38

Lab tests showed that Mark had a BAC of about .38—more than four times the legal limit.

Sadly, Mark passed away that morning.

How Alcohol Is Removed

You have learned how alcohol gets into the body. But, how is the alcohol removed? There are a lot of misconceptions about that. Try your hand at the activity below to see what you know.

Fact or myth? → Put a check next to each activity that you believe can help an intoxicated person become sober. Then, keep reading to find out whether you are correct or not.

1. _____ Drinking water

2. _____ Drinking coffee or energy drinks

3. _____ Taking vitamins or over-the-counter drugs

4. _____ Eating food

5. _____ Taking a cold shower

6. _____ Vomiting

7. _____ Switching to weaker drinks

8. _____ Exercising

9. _____ Urinating

Liver's role in removing alcohol. Many people believe that the activities in the previous Fact or Myth? question can actually sober them up. The fact is, the only thing that can break down alcohol in the bloodstream is the liver. And it can only do this so quickly.

Liver's speed in removing alcohol. The liver processes alcohol at a constant rate of about one drink per hour. This assumes that the person has a healthy liver. Diseased or damaged livers may process alcohol even more slowly.

FACTORS THAT AFFECT BLOOD ALCOHOL CONTENT (BAC)

Different factors can affect a person's BAC. You probably already know about some of these factors. Others may be surprising. Try the activity below and find out.

Who's BAC is higher? →

For each pair, circle the person who you think will have the higher BAC. After checking the answers, keep reading to learn why they are correct.

1.

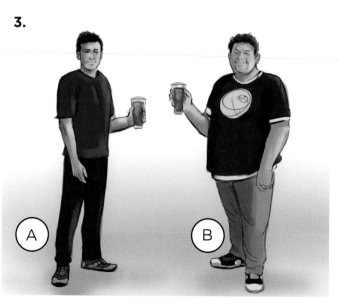

2.

3.

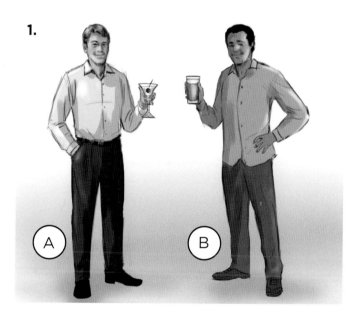

4.

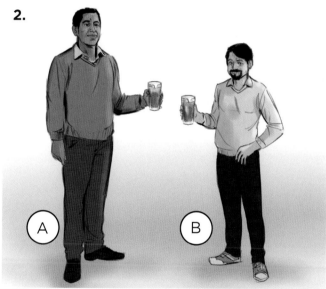

5.

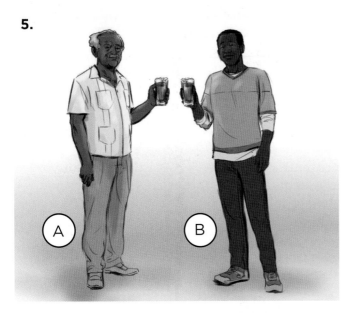

6.

7.

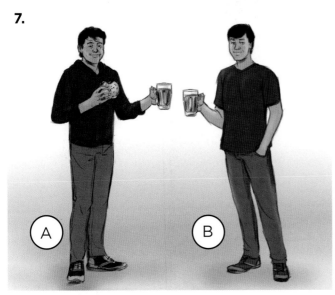

Drink Strength

The more alcohol a drink contains, the more that will end up in the bloodstream. This results in a higher BAC. For example, a martini generally contains more alcohol than a beer. So, if all other factors are the same, a martini drinker would have a higher BAC than a beer drinker.

Drink Quantity and Rate

BAC is also affected by how much a person drinks and how quickly. Remember, it takes the liver a whole hour to remove a single drink from the body. If a person drinks any more than that, the alcohol will build up in the bloodstream and raise the BAC.

Body Size

A small person will have a higher BAC than a large person, if all other factors are the same. That's because a small person's body has less blood to dilute the alcohol than a large person's body has. The more blood someone has, the more diluted the alcohol becomes.

Body Type

All other factors being the same, a person with a larger amount of body fat will have a higher BAC than a lean person. This is because body fat does not absorb alcohol. That means the alcohol has to stay in the bloodstream until the liver can break it down. In people with less body fat, alcohol can pass through muscle and spread throughout the body, giving them a lower BAC.

Gender

All other factors being the same, a woman will have a higher BAC than a man. That's because women:

- Generally have a higher percentage of body fat than men
- Have a smaller amount of an enzyme that helps break down alcohol
- Often are smaller than men and so have less blood in their bodies

Age

An older person will have a higher BAC than a younger person, all other factors being the same. Here is why:

- The enzymes that break down alcohol tend to slow as a person gets older.
- Body fat typically increases with age.

Food

A person who has not eaten will have a higher BAC than a person who has eaten, all other factors being the same. Food keeps alcohol in the stomach for a longer period of time. This slows the rate at which the food reaches the small intestine.

So, if you know a guest is dieting, take special care. The alcohol may pass more quickly through the stomach and into the small intestine, causing the guest to become intoxicated faster.

Carbonation

A person who is drinking a carbonated drink will have a higher BAC than a person whose drink is not carbonated, all other factors being the same. Carbonation speeds the rate at which alcohol passes from the stomach to the small intestine. This causes a person to reach a higher BAC at a faster rate.

Food Choices for Slowing the Absorption of Alcohol

Which food items are better for slowing the movement of alcohol? →

To keep alcohol in the stomach longer, any food is better than no food. Still, some types of food are better at doing this than others. See if you can identify which ones are better.

Place an X next to each food item that you believe is good for slowing the movement of alcohol to the small intestine. After checking the answers, keep reading to learn why they are correct.

1. _____ Cheese sticks

2. _____ Pretzel

3. _____ Bread

4. _____ Pizza

5. _____ Cheeseburger

6. _____ Chicken wings

Answers: 1, 4, 5, 6

When you know what makes a food item better or worse than another for slowing the movement of alcohol, you can suggest the best choices to guests.

Better food choices. These types of food are best because they take longer to digest:

● High-fat food—examples include pizza, chicken wings, nachos, and deep-fried items.

● High-protein food—examples include meat, fish, and eggs.

Poorer food choices. These types of food are not as good for slowing the movement of alocohol:

● High-carbohydrate food—these items are easily digested. They are less effective in slowing the movement of alcohol into the small intestine. Examples of high-carbohydrate-food items include bread and pasta.

● Salty food—these can make people thirsty. This may cause them to drink more alcohol. Examples of salty food include peanuts, pretzels, and chips.

Other Risk Factors for Intoxication

There are other risk factors for intoxication that you need to know about. These should be considered a red flag when you see them in people. If you see these risk factors, keep a close eye on your guests.

Feeling stressed, depressed, angry, or tired. People experiencing these emotions may be more susceptible to the effects of alcohol. The same is true for people who are tired when they arrive.

Taking medications or illegal drugs. People who drink alcohol while on medication or when using illegal drugs may experience:

● Dangerous drug-alcohol interactions

● Intensified effects

Suffering from certain health conditions. People with certain health conditions are more likely to feel the effects of alcohol. These conditions include:

● Transplant recipients

● Certain illnesses, such as cirrhosis of the liver or diabetes

Of course, it can be hard to tell if someone has a health condition just by looking at them. But sometimes they'll tell you about it as they drink. That's why listening to your guests is a valuable skill to develop.

Intent on becoming intoxicated. A person may also be a high-risk drinker based on why they are drinking. Certain events can trigger emotions that cause guests to drink more than they normally would. This can happen when drinking:

- To forget about a sad event, such as a funeral
- To celebrate a special event, such as a wedding
- To catch up to friends who have had more drinks
- While watching a sports event

Keep in mind that some people will be affected by a combination of conditions and factors. This means they are at an even higher risk for intoxication. These people will need even more attention to prevent intoxication.

ASSESSING A GUEST'S LEVEL OF INTOXICATION

When you know that a person is a high-risk drinker, you will need to watch that guest more closely. Doing this can help you prevent over-service. But the real key to preventing over-service is knowing how to assess a guest's level of intoxication.

How to assess a guest. A guest's level of intoxication can be assessed two ways:

1. Count the number of drinks you serve.
2. Observe the guest's behavior.

Using a combination of the two is the best approach for preventing over-service.

When should you assess a guest's level of intoxication? →

When to assess a guest. You should start assessing people from the time they enter the establishment and keep doing it until the time they leave. Watch a person's behavior when they arrive so you have a reference point. This will make it easier for you to spot changes in behavior.

Remember, your responsibility starts when you serve someone that first drink. And it continues for the entire time the person is on the premises, and even after they leave. If a person shows signs of intoxication or you are concerned about how many drinks they have had, it is your job to tell your manager and the appropriate coworkers and to stop service.

COUNTING DRINKS

Counting drinks can be useful for determining if a guest is intoxicated. This is especially true when the guest is not showing any signs of intoxication. But before you can count drinks, you first need to know what a drink is.

Drink Equivalencies

Standard measure of a drink. The following beverages serve as the standard measure for counting drinks. The sizes are very different, but they contain about the same amount of alcohol. Each is counted as one drink.

One Standard Drink

| 5 oz. | 12 oz. | 1.5 oz. | 1 oz. |
| Wine 12% | Beer 5% | 80-proof liquor | 100-proof liquor |

Remember, these are just the standard. Some beer, wine, and other alcoholic beverages have a higher alcohol content, so they must be counted differently.

Drink size and amount of alcohol. The size of a beverage and its contents also affect the way it is counted. That is because some beverages contain more alcohol than the standard drinks. So you will have to figure out the actual number of drinks in them. Sometimes, one beverage on a menu can equal several standard drinks!

3 Drinks

2 Drinks

Calculating Drinks

Does figuring out the number of standard drinks in a beverage sound complicated? Don't worry. Here is a simple formula to help you do this.

Amount of liquor in the beverage ÷ Amount of liquor in 1 standard drink = Number of drinks in beverage

Example 1. Suppose you need to calculate the drinks in a three-ounce glass of 80-proof whiskey. You would do it like this:

3 ounces of 80-proof whiskey ÷ 1.5 ounces of 80-proof liquor in 1 standard drink = 2 drinks

Your three-ounce glass of 80-proof whiskey—that single beverage—is actually two drinks.

Example 2. A 12-ounce beer with an ABV of 5% is counted as one drink. But suppose your establishment uses a 16-ounce pint glass for draft beer. The standard drinks in a 16-ounce beer would be calculated like this:

16 ounces of 5% beer ÷ 12 ounces of beer (5%) in 1 standard drink = 1.33 drinks

If you served a person three 16-ounce beers, you have really served them almost four drinks, not three.

Mixed Drinks

Mixed drinks often contain multiple liquors. Counting them can be a challenge, especially if the liquors each have different amounts of alcohol. But don't worry too much about the math. Most establishments make these calculations for you for each drink served. Always remember, though, that it's better to round up when counting drinks.

APPLY YOUR KNOWLEDGE

Calculating Drinks

Directions: Calculate the standard number of drinks in each beverage and select the correct answer.

---

60 oz. pitcher of beer, ABV 5%

1. How many drinks are contained in this pitcher?

    A. 3 drinks

    B. 4 drinks

    C. 5 drinks

    D. 6 drinks

---

15 oz. carafe of wine, ABV 12%

2. How many drinks are contained in this carafe?

    A. 3 drinks

    B. 4 drinks

    C. 5 drinks

    D. 6 drinks

---

2 oz. tequila (80 proof)
1 oz. Grand Marnier (80 proof)

3. How many drinks are contained in this margarita?

    A. 1 drink

    B. 2 drinks

    C. 3 drinks

    D. 4 drinks

---

1 oz. 100-proof bourbon
12 oz. beer, 5% ABV

4. How many drinks are contained in this order?

    A. 1 drink

    B. 2 drinks

    C. 3 drinks

    D. 4 drinks

For answers, see page 2-29.

ESTIMATING BAC

While you do not have to know a person's BAC, you do have to decide whether to continue serving alcohol. Being able to estimate BAC can help with this decision.

Follow these steps to estimate someone's BAC.

1. Count the number of standard drinks the person was served.

2. Estimate the person's weight.

3. Determine the person's BAC using a BAC chart.

BAC Charts

There are two different BAC charts—one for men and another for women (see page 2-20).

Basis for the BAC estimates. The estimates for the BAC charts on the next page are based on the following:

- Number of drinks consumed in one hour
- Assumption that a person's liver breaks down one drink per hour

What do the red cells on the BAC chart mean? →

The charts highlight BACs of .08 or higher by putting them in red. Remember, a BAC of .08 is the legal level of intoxication while driving in most states.

Limitation of BAC charts. The BAC charts can help you estimate someone's BAC with a reasonable degree of accuracy. But, a person's actual BAC may be higher or lower than what the chart says. That is because the charts cannot account for other factors that might affect a person; for example:

- Prior drinking
- Physical condition
- Emotional state
- Whether someone has eaten or taken medication

Due to this limitation, BAC charts should only be used as a reference.

Using BAC Charts

As stated earlier, you need two pieces of information before using a BAC chart: how many standard drinks a person has had and the person's estimated weight. Then do this:

1. Go to the row for the number of drinks.

2. Follow the row across until you have reached the column with the person's estimated weight.

3. Where the row and column meet, you will find the person's BAC.

Body Weight

# of Drinks	100 lbs.	120 lbs.	140 lbs.	160 lbs.	180 lbs.	200 lbs.	220 lbs.	240 lbs.
1	.022	.015	.011	.007	.005	.003	.001	.000
2	.059	.046	.038	.031	.026	.022	.018	.015
3	.097	.078	.064	.054	.046	.040	.035	.031
4	.134	.109	.091	.078	.067	.059	.052	.046
5	.172	.140	.118	.101	.088	.078	.069	.062
6	.209	.172	.145	.125	.109	.097	.086	.078
7	.247	.203	.172	.148	.130	.115	.103	.093
8	.284	.234	.198	.172	.151	.134	.120	.109

■ Indicates a BAC of .08 or higher

Body Weight

# of Drinks	100 lbs.	120 lbs.	140 lbs.	160 lbs.	180 lbs.	200 lbs.	220 lbs.	240 lbs.
1	.029	.022	.016	.012	.009	.006	.004	.003
2	.074	.059	.048	.040	.034	.029	.025	.022
3	.119	.097	.080	.068	.059	.052	.045	.040
4	.164	.134	.113	.096	.084	.074	.066	.059
5	.209	.172	.145	.125	.109	.097	.086	.078
6	.254	.209	.177	.153	.134	.119	.107	.097
7	.299	.247	.209	.181	.159	.142	.127	.115
8	.344	.284	.241	.209	.184	.164	.148	.134

■ Indicates a BAC of .08 or higher

APPLY YOUR KNOWLEDGE

Using a BAC Chart

Directions: For each scenario, use the appropriate BAC chart on page 2-20 to determine the person's BAC and whether he or she is at or above the legal limit for driving. Write your answers in the space provided.

1. A 240-pound man had four 12-ounce beers at 5% ABV in one hour.

   What is his estimated BAC? _____

   Is he at or above the legal limit for driving? (Yes/No) _____

2. A 140-pound woman had three five-ounce glasses of wine at 12% ABV in one hour.

   What is her estimated BAC? _____

   Is she at or above the legal limit for driving? (Yes/No) _____

For the answers, see page 2-29.

TRACKING DRINK COUNTS

To estimate a person's BAC, you need to know how many drinks the person has consumed.

Ways to Track Drinks

There are many ways to track the number of drinks that someone has had. Which way is best for you depends on the type of establishment you work in and how busy you are. Here are some possibilities:

- Use a physical tally sheet.
- Mark drinks on a coaster or napkin as shown in the photo at left.
- Place a printed receipt in front of the guest, and update it each time the guest is served another drink.
- Use the point-of-sale system.
- Keep a drink tally on the back of the guest check.

In some establishments, the guest check moves with the guest, which makes counting easier.

Regardless of the method, you should share drink counts with other staff members and serving stations. Remember, tracking drinks is a shared responsibility.

Special Challenges to Tracking Drinks

Some situations may make it difficult to track drink counts.

Self-Service

Tracking drink counts is a common problem in self-service situations like these:

- Bottle service. With bottle service, bottles of liquor are sold to a table of guests, along with the necessary mixers, garnishes, and other supplies. Then guests can mix their own drinks.
- Tableside dispensers. With tableside beer and wine dispensers, guests serve themselves beer or wine.

Establishments that offer self-service opportunities must create policies to monitor guests—and then stick to the policies. For example, some bottle service establishments will assign a host to the table to make drinks using the guest's liquor bottles and mixers. This allows the host to count each guest's drinks.

What are some ways to avoid over-pouring? →

Over-Pouring

Over-pouring is another troublesome problem. This is when you add extra liquor to a beverage. For example, say the recipe for a gin and tonic calls for one and a half ounces of 80-proof gin. During a guest's visit, you mix three gin and tonics for the guest. But you pour an extra half ounce of gin in each drink. This means that you have actually served that guest four drinks instead of three.

Accurate drink-counting requires bartenders to know and closely follow drink recipes. And they should be tested on that knowledge. That includes using the right-size glass when making drinks and not overfilling them. This is especially important when pouring a glass of wine, as it can be easy to overfill the glass.

OBSERVING GUESTS FOR SIGNS OF INTOXICATION

You can learn a lot about how alcohol is affecting people by watching them.

Change in behavior. Look for physical and behavioral changes in your guests. A change in behavior is more revealing than the actual behavior itself. There is a big difference between a normally loud guest and one who is quiet at first but becomes loud after a few drinks.

Communicate with guests. Keep talking to each guest throughout his or her stay. By talking with guests, you can get a better idea of why they are there and whether or not they are becoming intoxicated. This communication is important.

Signs of Intoxication

When large amounts of alcohol reach the brain, it stops functioning normally. This causes physical and behavioral changes including:

What are the signs of intoxication? →

- Relaxed inhibitions
- Impaired judgment
- Slowed reaction time
- Impaired motor coordination

Relaxed Inhibitions

Inhibitions prevent people from saying or doing things that may be unacceptable to others. As people drink, their normal inhibitions become relaxed. Guests with relaxed inhibitions may show these behaviors:

- Be overly friendly
- Be unfriendly, depressed, or quiet
- Become loud
- Make rude comments
- Use foul language

Impaired Judgment

As people drink, the alcohol starts to impair their judgment. They lose the ability to make sensible decisions. Guests with impaired judgment may show these behaviors:

- Complain about the strength of a drink after drinking others of the same strength
- Begin drinking faster or switch to larger or stronger drinks
- Make irrational or argumentative statements
- Become careless with money, such as buying drinks for strangers

Slowed Reaction Time

Guests' reaction time and responses will become slower as they drink. Guests with slowed reaction time may show these behaviors:

- Talk or move slowly
- Be unable to concentrate, lose their train of thought, or become forgetful
- Become drowsy
- Become glassy eyed, lose eye contact, or become unable to focus

Impaired Motor Coordination

Guests' motor skills will be affected as they drink. People with impaired motor coordination are easier to spot because they show the classic signs of intoxication. Guests with impaired motor coordination may show these behaviors:

- Stagger, stumble, fall down, bump objects, or sway when sitting or standing
- Be unable to pick up objects or may drop them
- Spill drinks or miss their mouths when drinking
- Slur their speech

Most people know when they see someone with impaired motor coordination that the person is intoxicated. But some of the other signs of intoxication are harder to spot, especially if there hasn't been enough time to see a change in the person's behavior. Not surprisingly, it is the subtle signs that you really have to watch for.

Does having a
tolerance to
alcohol affect a
person's BAC? →

Tolerance to Alcohol

Some people can handle the effects of alcohol without showing the usual signs. In fact, many experienced drinkers can drink quite a bit of alcohol without showing any signs. This ability, or tolerance to alcohol, does not affect a person's BAC at all.

How can you tell if an experienced drinker is intoxicated? You have to count their drinks.

Can people show signs
of intoxication after
having only one drink?
→

Inexperienced Drinkers

In contrast, people who are not experienced drinkers often show signs of intoxication after drinking only a small amount of alcohol. Their bodies are not used to it, so they are sensitive to smaller amounts.

APPLY YOUR KNOWLEDGE

Is this Person Intoxicated?

Directions: Watch each video scenario provided by your instructor and decide whether the guest or guests are intoxicated. Circle the correct answer.

Scenario		Are They Intoxicated?	
1.	A woman ordering a drink from a bartender.	Yes	No
2.	A regular drinking at the bar.	Yes	No
3.	Lawyers drinking at a dining table.	Yes	No
4.	A man getting a divorce drinking at the bar.	Yes	No
5.	A woman drinking at a wine bar.	Yes	No

For answers, see page 2-29.

PREVENTING GUESTS FROM BECOMING INTOXICATED

As a seller or server of alcohol, one of your most important jobs is to do everything possible to prevent guests from becoming intoxicated. Doing this may be easier said than done. However, there are some simple practices you can do to help your guests drink responsibly and provide good service.

Offer Water

One simple thing that helps keep guests from becoming intoxicated is to offer them water. Drinking alcohol causes dehydration. This can cause guests to drink more than they ordinarily would. Offering water and refilling water glasses frequently relieves both problems. It helps keep guests hydrated, and it may reduce the amount of alcohol they drink.

Offer Food

Another way to prevent intoxication is to offer food. Remember, food keeps alcohol in the stomach for a longer period of time, slowing its movement into the small intestine—and, more importantly, the bloodstream. Any food is better than no food. But for best results, offer food high in fat or protein, and avoid suggesting carbohydrates and salty food.

Offer Nonalcoholic Drinks

Offer your guests nonalcoholic drinks as an alternative to alcohol. This allows people who have had service stopped feel like they are still part of the group.

Measure Liquor

You can also help prevent intoxication by paying attention to how drinks are poured and mixed.

Ways to measure liquor. Measuring liquor is the best way to prevent over-pouring. Here are a few tools to help with this:

- Jiggers.
- Mechanical pour spouts.
- Technology-equipped pour spouts. Many of these devices connect to the point-of-sale (POS) system and can even aid in inventory control.

Ways to control free-pouring. In establishments where bartenders free-pour, management should make sure that free-pouring is done accurately:

- Train bartenders to free-pour accurately.
- Regularly check their accuracy using pour tests.

Set Drink Limits

Some establishments limit the number of drinks that will be served to a guest. For example, management may set a maximum number of drinks that can be served to each guest per hour. These limits slow drinking, which can help prevent intoxication.

MENU

Margarita $8.50

Moscow Mule $9.50

Mojito $9.50

Cosmopolitan $8.50

Pina Colada $8.50

Classic Manhattan $9.00

Hurricane $8.50

Whiskey Sour $8.25

Gin Fizz $8.25

Strawberry Daiquri $8.50

**We can only serve you
2 drinks per hour**

SELF-CHECK

Directions: Read the question and choose the best answer.

1. **Most of the alcohol a person drinks is absorbed into the bloodstream from what organ?**

   A. Liver

   B. Mouth

   C. Stomach

   D. Small intestine

2. **How many drinks can the liver break down in one hour?**

   A. 1

   B. 2

   C. 3

   D. 4

3. **What's the percentage of alcohol contained in a bottle of 80-proof whiskey?**

   A. 20%

   B. 40%

   C. 60%

   D. 80%

4. **In most states, it is illegal to drive a car with a BAC of**

   A. .02.

   B. .04.

   C. .06.

   D. .08.

5. **All other factors being equal, which person will have the highest BAC after two drinks?**

   A. A slim 26-year-old man

   B. A slim 28-year-old woman

   C. A slightly overweight 49-year-old man

   D. A slightly overweight 54-year-old woman

6. **Which food is best for slowing the movement of alcohol into the small intestine?**

   A. Pizza

   B. Popcorn

   C. Pretzels

   D. Dinner rolls

7. **Which behavior is a sign that a guest is experiencing relaxed inhibitions?**

   A. Slurring speech

   B. Becoming drowsy

   C. Making rude comments

   D. Swaying when standing

8. **Which behavior is a sign that a guest is experiencing impaired judgment?**

   A. Talking slowly

   B. Drinking faster

   C. Being overly-friendly

   D. Making rude comments

9. **Which behavior is a sign that a guest is experiencing slowed reaction time?**

   A. Losing eye contact

   B. Using foul language

   C. Bumping into objects

   D. Becoming careless with money

10. **Which behavior is a sign that a guest is experiencing impaired motor coordination?**

    A. Spilling drinks

    B. Becoming quiet

    C. Becoming forgetful

    D. Becoming depressed

For answers, see page 2-30.

Answer Key

Apply Your Knowledge: Calculating Drinks

1. **C.** Divide 60 ounces by 12, the amount of beer in one standard drink, to get five drinks.

2. **A.** Divide 15 ounces by 5 ounces, the amount of wine in one standard drink, to get three drinks.

3. **B.** Divide 3 ounces by 1.5 ounces, the amount of 80-proof liquor in one standard drink, to get two drinks.

4. **B.** One ounce of 100-proof bourbon is one standard drink. The 12-ounce beer is another standard drink. This gives a total of 2 drinks.

Apply Your Knowledge: Using a BAC Chart

1. The man's estimated BAC is .046. No, he is not at or above the legal limit for driving.

2. The woman's estimated BAC is .080. Yes, she is at or above the legal limit for driving.

Apply Your Knowledge: Is this Person Intoxicated?

1. **Yes**, she is intoxicated. She is complaining about the strength of her drink after drinking others of the same strength. She is also argumentative. These are signs of impaired judgement. She also made several rude comments, which may be a sign of relaxed inhibitions.

2. **Yes**, he is intoxicated. He is drinking fast, and he wants to switch to a double—a much stronger drink. These are classic signs of impaired judgment.

3. **No**, they do not seem to be intoxicated. Even though it looks like they have each had a few drinks, there are no outward signs of intoxication. They are eating, which slows down the rate at which the alcohol gets into their bloodstream. They are also working, which makes it likely that they have been there for a while, giving their bodies more time to process the drinks.

4. **No**, he is not intoxicated, at least not at this point. He is a big man, and he has only had two shots so far. But his rate of drinking and his emotional state are a concern. He needs to be watched closely.

5. **Yes,** she is definitely intoxicated. She showed classic signs that her reaction time was being affected by the alcohol. She was moving slowly when she set the glass down and she had trouble focusing to read the text. She also showed signs of impaired motor coordination: almost knocking over the glass, having difficulty picking up the phone and texting, and slurring her speech.

Self-Check

1. D
2. A
3. B
4. D
5. D
6. A
7. C
8. B
9. A
10. A

Notes

CHAPTER 3

Checking Identification

How do you feel about checking IDs?

"Checking IDs makes me nervous. I mean, let's be real; when someone has an out-of-state ID, I don't always know what to look for. What if I mess up?"

"Look, I'm 21. Sometimes I have to card people who are the same age as I am—or even older. It's embarrassing."

"Mostly I've gotten used to carding. But when someone gets mad about it, it's really frustrating. I'm just doing my job."

OBJECTIVES

After completing this chapter, you will be able to identify the following:

- When to check IDs
- Which types of ID are acceptable
- What makes an ID valid
- The signs of a fake or altered ID
- How to determine if a person is 21 or older
- How to determine if an ID belongs to the person who gave it

There is a lot you need to know to avoid serving alcohol to someone who is underage. Unfortunately, fake identification (ID) can be tough to spot. And younger people sometimes look a lot older than they actually are. This is especially true for young women.

Who's 21 or older? →

For example, while the women in these photos look old enough to drink, only one is. Can you tell which one? Circle the correct answer.

A

B

Answer: A

Even if you correctly guessed which woman is old enough to be served, hopefully this exercise made you think. Serving alcohol based on a hunch about someone's age is dangerous and irresponsible. The penalties can be severe, and you could put people in danger, too. Are you willing to do that based on how old you think someone looks? Of course not!

That's where this chapter comes in. Here you will learn when and how to check IDs.

WHEN TO CHECK IDs

NOTICE

WE CARD EVERYONE UNDER 30

Should you recheck the ID of someone who has already been carded? →

You are responsible for making sure your guests are at least 21 years old before you sell or serve them alcohol. If you are not sure that a guest is old enough, you must ask for an ID.

Follow company policies and local laws. Unfortunately, it may not always be obvious when to check IDs. Some states and establishments take the guesswork out of carding by providing specific guidelines. For example, if someone looks older than 21 but younger than 30, you might have to check ID. The best way to keep yourself and others safe is to always follow your company policy and state and local laws.

Check the ID of any guest you are unsure about. You should check the ID of any guest whose age you are unsure about, even if the guest was already carded by a coworker. It is not safe to assume that guests are old enough to drink even if they have drink tickets, are wearing a wrist band, or have a stamp to indicate that they were carded. Also, it is a good idea to card guests if they leave and then return.

Do NOT allow underage guests to be served. If you allow a guest who you know is underage to be served alcohol by a coworker, you can be held liable. This is true even if the guest presented what appears to be a genuine ID.

Communicate with your team. When underage guests are attempting to drink, communication among staff is critical. Remember, it is everyone's responsibility to make sure that alcohol is not served to guests under the age of 21.

HOW TO CHECK IDs

When you check an ID, there are several things you should look for before accepting it:

- The ID is acceptable.
- The ID is valid.
- The ID has not been falsified or altered.
- The guest is old enough to be served alcohol.
- The ID belongs to the guest.

Once you have determined the ID is an acceptable type, you can check the other items in any order. More details follow on each of these.

Hold the ID and Check Both Sides

Can you accept an ID that's shown to you in a wallet? →

Holding an ID is really important. **NEVER** let a guest just show you an ID or leave it in their wallet. You need to hold the ID so that you can see both sides up close and feel it. This helps you make sure that it is real and not altered.

If a guest shows you an ID that is still in a wallet, politely ask the guest to remove the ID and hand it to you. If the guest asks why, apologize and explain that it is company policy.

Types of Acceptable ID

Getting an ID in your hands is just the first step in checking an ID. You also have to know whether you can accept it for proof of age. This depends on the laws in your area. For example, some areas do not allow out-of-state drivers' licenses or state ID cards to be used for alcohol service. Others do.

If you're not sure which types of IDs are acceptable where you work, check with your manager.

Most states accept the same types of IDs. You probably already know some of them, but see if you can identify all of them.

Which IDs are acceptable? →

Put a check next to each type of ID that is accepted in most states for proof of age. After checking the answers, talk to your manager to learn which IDs are acceptable in your establishment.

1. _____ State identification card

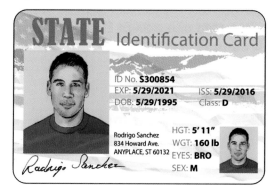

2. _____ School identification card

3. _____ Passport

4. _____ Birth certificate

5. _____ Military identification card

6. _____ Driver's license

7. _____ Permanent resident card

Answers: 1, 3, 5, and 6 are accepted in most states. 7 depends on the area. Ask your manager if a permanent resident card is acceptable in your area.

If you are not familiar with some of these IDs, you should use an ID checking guide to validate them. (This guide is covered later.)

Making Sure an ID Is Valid

An ID must be valid before you can accept it. That means it has all the parts that it should.

A valid ID has the following features.

Owner's photo. The photo is used to verify that the person who presented the ID is the owner.

Current (not expired). In most states an expired license is not valid. This helps prevent an underage person from using it.

Owner's birthdate. The birthdate can be used to calculate the age of the guest. However, most state-issued IDs now include the date an underage person will turn 21.

Owner's signature. The signature can be used to verify that the person who presented it is the owner.

Intact. In most states, a damaged ID is not valid and cannot be accepted. Damage could have been caused by someone altering the ID.

Making Sure an ID Is Real and Not Altered

Part of checking an ID is determining whether it appears to be real. Unfortunately, fake IDs are becoming more common. Many of them are pretty convincing.

So how do you know if an ID is real or not? The key is knowing what a real ID is supposed to look like. This may not always be simple, but it can be done. You just need the right knowledge and the right tools.

ID Checking Guide

One of the most important tools for checking IDs is an ID checking guide. These guides provide samples and descriptions of current drivers' licenses and state ID cards. They also include detailed descriptions of security features on each ID.

If you are a manager, keep the following in mind:

- Have ID checking guides available for staff. Make sure they know where these guides are located. Consider placing a guide at each point-of-sale (POS) terminal.
- Make sure the ID checking guide you are using is current. These guides are issued annually.
- Make sure appropriate staff are trained on how to use these guides.

Security Features

Other tools used in recognizing fake or altered IDs are security features. Government agencies use them on IDs to make them harder to alter or fake. Some examples follow.

Text and images that can only be seen under ultraviolet light.

Special surfaces on the laminate or other treatments that give the ID a specific texture, thickness, or flexibility.

Text or images that change color or appear to move when the ID is turned or rotated.

Ghost photos, which are smaller, less clear copies of the person's photo placed on the ID.

Microprinting, which is text placed on the ID that is too small to read with the naked eye.

Format—In most states, the IDs issued to people younger than 21 are in a vertical format rather than the horizontal format used for those 21 or older.

Can a person with a vertical format ID be 21 or older? →

Keep in mind that IDs do not always expire on the person's birthday. So a person who gives you a vertical format ID may actually have turned 21. Check the ID carefully. If the guest has turned 21 and the ID is not expired, it may be okay to serve that person assuming everything else checks out okay.

Is it okay to accept an ID that is blank on the back? →

Back of the ID

All government-issued ID cards have information on the back. A majority of states include bar codes, magnetic stripes, or both. These contain specific data about the person, which can be accessed using an ID reader.

The backs of fake IDs are sometimes blank, so be sure to check the back of all IDs.

Signs of Tampering

Once you have an ID in your hands, look at it closely. Remember, in most states, a damaged ID is not valid. If you find any damage or signs of tampering, do **NOT** accept the ID.

Look for these signs of tampering:

- **Surface issues.** The surface is **NOT** how it should be for the type of ID, such as smooth, embossed, or textured. Use an ID checking guide to see what to expect.
- **Lamination flaws.** The lamination has flaws, such as holes, cuts, tears, or bubbles.
- **Rough edges.** The edges are rough rather than smooth.
- **Blurry or raised photos.** The photo is blurry or has raised edges. Either can mean someone added a new photo.
- **Thickness.** The ID is too thick or too thin. If it is too thick it might mean someone added layers to hide something.

Additional Tools for Checking IDs

Several tools can make the task of checking IDs easier. You may already be familiar with some of these tools.

Which tool should you use? →

See if you can match the ID checking tool to its best use. Place the correct letter in the blank space next to its corresponding number. After checking the answers, keep reading to find out why they are correct.

Tool	Best Use?
1. _____ Ultraviolet (UV) light	A. Showing microprinting
2. _____ Magnifying glass	B. Verifying a guest's age
3. _____ Flashlight	C. Showing pin holes or cuts
4. _____ ID reader	D. Showing text and images that only appear under special light

Answers: 1. D, 2. A, 3. C, 4. B

Best uses of tools. Here are some tools for checking IDs and the best ways to use them:

Ultraviolet lights show security features that do not appear under regular light.

Magnifying glasses can be used to see microprinting on an ID.

Flashlights can be used to backlight IDs. This reveals pin holes, cut marks, and other signs of tampering.

ID readers show the card holder's age and other information from the ID's magnetic stripes or bar codes.

These tools should only be used to help with the ID-checking process. They should **NEVER** replace a good, thorough inspection.

Best practices for ID readers. When using ID readers, keep these things in mind:

- Always compare the readout with the information on the ID. If the information does not match, the ID is a fake or was altered.

What should you do if an ID reader can't read an ID? →

- If the ID reader gives an error code, check the magnetic stripe or bar codes. People sometimes scratch them to stump the ID reader, as shown below. If there are scratches, politely ask for another valid form of ID.

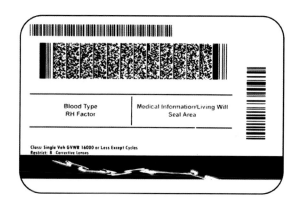

Dealing with a Fake or Altered ID

When someone uses a fake or altered ID, you cannot serve them alcohol. And depending on the rules of your establishment and state and local law, you might also have to take one or more of these actions:

- Refuse entry to the establishment.
- Confiscate the ID, if required.
- Call the police, if required.

Always follow your company policy and the law in your area.

Making Sure the Guest Is Old Enough to Drink

There is still one more thing to check on an ID: whether the guest is 21 or older.

While most state-issued IDs show when someone underage will turn 21 years old, you still need to know how to calculate a person's age to see if they are 21 or older. To do this:

1. **Add 21 to the person's birth year.**
   To make this easier, you could add 20 to the birth year and then add 1 to the total. The calculated year plus the person's birthday—the month and day—tell you when the person turns 21.

2. **Determine if the person's birthday has passed.**
   Compare the current date to the calculated date when the person will turn 21—the month, day, and year. If the person's birthday has passed, the person is 21 or older. If it has not passed, the person is underage. Here is an example:

   DOB: 06/15/1996
   +21

   Age 21 on 6/15/2017

   Current date
   7/15/17
   vs
   Calculated 21 birthdate **>** **21 or older**
   6/15/2017

YOU MUST BE 21

YOUR BIRTH DATE MUST BE ON OR BEFORE TODAY'S DATE IN

1998

TO PURCHASE ALCOHOLIC BEVERAGES

Some establishments post signs or calendars stating that a guest must have been born on or before a certain date to be served alcohol. These can be really helpful in determining if a guest is old enough to drink.

APPLY YOUR KNOWLEDGE

Old Enough to Drink?

Directions: Assume you are checking IDs on April 3, 2019. Use the birthdates on the IDs below to determine if each person is 21 or older. Circle the correct answer.

Birthdate	On April 3, 2019, Is This Person 21 or Older?

1.

   Yes

   No

2.

   Yes

   No

3.

   Yes

   No

For answers, see page 3-18.

Make Sure the ID Belongs to the Person

What if an underage guest uses the valid ID of an older family member or friend? Or what if they use the expired license of an older person who has been issued a new one? This is a pretty common practice. The way to combat it is to make sure the ID actually belongs to the person who gave it to you. Here's how to do that.

Compare the Person to the ID Photo

Compare the person who gives you the ID to the photo on the ID. Look at these features that usually do not change over time:

- Shape of the chin
- Shape of the head
- Distance between the eyes
- Location and shape of the ears
- Distance between the eyebrows and hairline
- Visible scars

Compare the Person to the Physical Traits on the ID

Physical traits can change over time. Even so, many of them can still be used to help determine if the ID belongs to the person who presented it. Look at the following traits on the ID to see if they match the person.

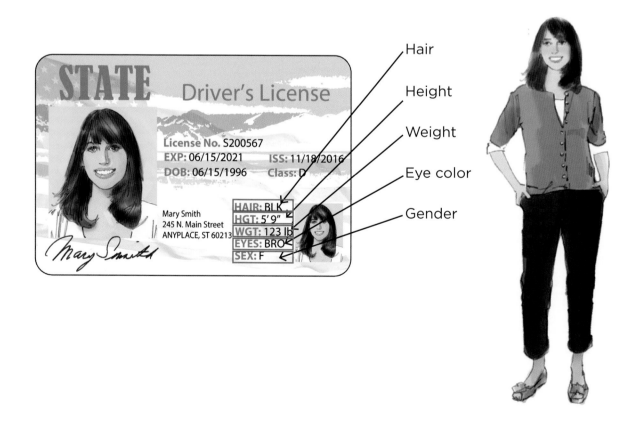

What if you're not sure that an ID belongs to someone? →

Ask for More Proof

If you still have doubts about whether an ID belongs to someone, ask the person for another ID. Any of the acceptable types discussed earlier will work. However, some establishments will accept something of value with a person's name on it as a second form of identification, like a credit or debit card. Talk to your manager to see if this is okay.

If you are still having doubts about the person who handed you the ID, there are a couple more things you can do:

- Ask the person questions that the ID owner should know. This might include questions like:

  » What is your address?

  » What is your birthdate or age?

  » How tall are you?

  » What is your middle name?

  If the person hesitates while answering any of these questions, they may not be the owner of the ID.

- Ask guests to sign their name on a piece of paper. Then compare the person's signature to the signature on the ID.

APPLY YOUR KNOWLEDGE

Did They Handle It Correctly?

Directions: Watch each video scenario provided by the instructor and decide whether the employee handled the situation correctly. Circle the correct answer.

Video Scenario	Description	Was the Situation Handled Correctly?
1.	Young guest orders at a bar.	Yes No
2.	Door person cards young guests.	Yes No
3.	Young couple orders drinks at a restaurant.	Yes No
4.	Family wants to share a bottle of wine.	Yes No
5.	Door person scans IDs.	Yes No

For answers, see page 3-18.

SELF-CHECK

Directions: Read the question and choose the best answer.

1. **Which type of ID is acceptable for verifying a guest's age?**

   A. Passport

   B. School ID

   C. Birth certificate

   D. Voter registration card

2. **A valid ID must have a/an**

   A. photo.

   B. address.

   C. textured surface.

   D. image that moves or changes color.

3. **Which feature is commonly used on IDs for someone younger than 21?**

   A. A bar code

   B. A ghost photo

   C. A vertical format

   D. A horizontal format

4. **Comparing an ID photo to the guest is one way to determine that the**

   A. ID is real.

   B. guest is intoxicated.

   C. ID belongs to the guest.

   D. guest is old enough to drink.

5. **Which shows that an ID has been altered or is fake?**

   A. ID is expired

   B. Format is horizontal

   C. Back of the ID is blank

   D. Photo is not of the guest

For answers, see page 3-18.

Answer Key

Apply Your Knowledge: Old Enough to Drink?

1. **Yes.** This guest turned 21 on November 30, 2018.

1. **No.** This guest will not turn 21 until May 17, 2019.

2. **Yes.** This guest turned 21 on March 6, 2019.

Apply Your Knowledge: Did They Handle It Correctly?

1. **No.** The bartender should have asked the person to take her ID out of the wallet and hand it to him. Then he should have spent more time checking the front and back of the ID and comparing it to the person.

2. **Yes.** The door person thoroughly checked the ID—front and back—then compared it to the person to make sure it belonged to him. When the door person was unsure about that, he asked questions the ID owner should know and had the person write his signature.

3. **Yes.** The server checked the IDs thoroughly making sure they belonged to the people and were acceptable and genuine. When he saw that one person's license had expired, which made it invalid, he correctly asked for another valid form of ID.

4. **Yes.** The server did the right thing by rejecting the college ID and asking for another acceptable form of ID.

5. **No.** While the door person did scan the licenses with an ID reader, he did not make sure that the readout matched the information on the licenses. He also failed to do a good, thorough inspection of the ID.

Self-Check

1. A

2. A

3. C

4. C

5. C

Notes

_____
_____
_____
_____
_____
_____
_____
_____
_____
_____
_____
_____
_____
_____
_____
_____
_____
_____
_____
_____
_____
_____
_____
_____
_____
_____
_____

CHAPTER 4

Handling Difficult Situations

How do you feel about stopping service?

"I'm not going to lie, it can be scary. But I just remind myself that it's the right thing to do."

"I never know how people will react. Sometimes it's okay. Sometimes they get mad or abusive."

"It just comes with the territory. I've been doing this for a while, so I know it's just got to be done sometimes."

OBJECTIVES

After completing this chapter, you will be able to identify the following:

- How to deal with intoxicated guests
- Ways to communicate in difficult situations
- How to handle potentially violent situations and violence
- How to handle illegal activities
- What to do when people present fake or altered IDs
- What to do when law enforcement or liquor authorities visit your establishment

Some of the difficult situations that you encounter on the job may feel uncomfortable. Some may even be scary. Fortunately, there are some simple steps and techniques you can learn to resolve these situations as painlessly as possible.

FUNDAMENTALS FOR SAFETY

When learning and applying the steps and techniques in this chapter, always keep safety and the requirements of your establishment in mind.

Personal safety first. Personal safety must always come first. If you believe that you or others are at risk, call the police. **NEVER** assume an unsafe situation will resolve itself, because it usually won't.

Follow the requirements for your establishment. Keep in mind that this course is providing general information for handling difficult situations. Different establishments may have their own rules. Also, sometimes what you need to do will depend on local laws.

Whatever you do, always follow your company policy and the laws in your area.

DEALING WITH INTOXICATED GUESTS

When people drink too much, you have to stop serving them alcohol. When and how you do this can make a big difference in the outcome.

But stopping alcohol service is only one aspect of dealing with intoxicated guests. For example, you may stop service to a guest and later find that the guest has been given a drink by a friend. Or you might learn that an intoxicated guest plans to drive. And what about guests who are already intoxicated when they arrive? Luckily, some of the steps and techniques you will learn for stopping service can also be applied to other difficult situations.

When to Stop Service

Remember, there are two situations when you have to stop serving someone alcohol:

- The person is showing signs of intoxication.
- You are concerned about the number of drinks the person has had. (This is where knowing the BAC chart comes in handy.)

Who Can Stop Service

Are you allowed to stop service? →

Some establishments allow employees to stop service but require them to notify a manager. Other places require managers to stop service. Make sure you know and follow your company policy.

When to Tell the Person

When is the best time to tell someone you're stopping alcohol service? →

The best time to tell someone that you have to stop service is when the person wants to order the next drink. This is the better time to tell someone because stopping service can upset people. If you tell your guests as you serve their final drink, there is more time for their resentment to build while they continue to drink.

Always remember, though, that if you see that a person is becoming intoxicated, you must stop service immediately. In some areas, this might mean stopping service while the person is still finishing a drink. Refer to your company policy and state and local laws.

How to Stop Service

Stopping alcohol service involves more than just telling the guest that you have to stop service. To keep everyone safe, there are steps you should take both before and after this conversation.

1. Alert a Backup

Before stopping service, ask your manager or another coworker to back you up. The backup person must be:

- Available to help, if needed
- Close enough to see and hear what's happening
- Not so close that the guest feels threatened

2. Ask for Help if Possible

If there's an opportunity to do so, ask the intoxicated guest's friends or relatives for help. They might be able to convince the person not to order another drink. They can also help smooth things over.

If you plan to ask for this type of support, wait until the intoxicated person steps away.

3. Tell the Person

When telling someone that you cannot serve them anymore:

- Always be professional and polite.
- Be aware of your body language. Do **NOT** frown or stare. This can be interpreted as shaming or aggression, and it may escalate things.
- Remain calm, even if the person does not.
- Do **NOT** get personal or take anything personally.

To help you become more comfortable with this step, some communication techniques are detailed later.

4. Offer Food and Nonalcoholic Alternatives

After telling the person that you have to stop service, offer food and nonalcoholic alternatives. They are helpful for a few reasons:

- If the person is there with others, having a nonalcoholic drink or food may let the person still feel like part of the group.

- Food slows the movement of alcohol into the bloodstream by keeping it in the stomach. Fatty, high-protein food does this best, but other types of food can still help.

- The longer a guest sits there not drinking alcohol, the more time the body has to process the alcohol that was already consumed.

Are intoxicated people allowed to remain in your establishment? →

Be aware that in some states it is against the law to let an intoxicated person stay on the property. Before offering food and nonalcoholic drinks, confirm that this is actually an option for you. As always, follow the law and company policy.

5. Tell Your Coworkers

Once you have stopped service to a guest, make sure all of your coworkers in the front of the house know. This means everyone—bartenders and servers, hosts, coat check attendants, security, valets, and others. Why? Because others from your team might be needed to keep the guest from drinking more or driving while intoxicated.

Communication Techniques for Difficult Situations

The hardest part of stopping service is telling the guest. But there are some communication techniques that you can use to help make this and other difficult situations easier.

Avoid Judgmental Language

No one wants to feel judged. If you use judgmental language when you stop service, it is more likely to upset your guest.

Which statement is judgmental? →

What is judgmental language? Take a look at these statements and see if you can tell. Circle the correct answer.

A.   "Sorry, but you've had enough."

B.   "Sorry, but it's against the law for me to serve you any more alcohol."

Answer: A

The first statement is judgmental because it sounds like you personally think the guest has had too much to drink. The second is stated as a fact: the law requires you to stop serving alcohol.

To avoid using judgmental language:

- Avoid "you" statements. Statements that start with the word "you," such as, "You've had enough," can cause problems. They invite argument and can also offend the person.

- Explain with facts. Cite the law or company policy. This deflects blame and keeps things from getting personal.

- Here are some examples:

  » "Our company policy doesn't allow me to serve you any more alcohol."

  » "It's against the law for me to serve you any more alcohol."

Pick one or two statements like these that work for you. Practice them until you feel comfortable saying them.

Express Concern

People are more likely to respond positively when they think you are stopping service out of concern for them. But it needs to be genuine.

Which statement expresses concern? →

Which statement do you think shows concern for the guest? Circle the correct answer.

    A. "I just want to make sure you get home okay."

    B. "Sorry, but I'm just trying to do my job."

Answer: A

The first statement tells the person that you care about him or her. In this example, you are showing concern for the person's safety. The second statement does not express any concern for the person. It is not bad on its own; it just does not show concern.

Express Empathy

Empathy means putting yourself in someone else's shoes. When you express empathy, you let the person know that you understand their situation and how he or she feels. We all appreciate a little understanding. That's why expressing empathy is a good practice in many difficult conversations.

Which statement expresses empathy? →

Can you tell which statement expresses empathy for the guest? Circle the correct answer.

    A. "I'm sorry if this is upsetting."

    B. "I'm sorry, but I just can't serve you another one."

Answer: A

The first statement lets the person know that you understand how they feel. While the second statement is not bad to say, it does not express empathy.

Be Firm

You have to be firm when stopping service. Backing down after attempting to stop service does not do anyone any favors. In fact, it is against the law. Plus, you will train your guests to disregard you. Then next time it will be even harder to stop service.

Which statement expresses that you are being firm? →

Which statement is an example of being firm? Circle the correct answer.

    A. "Okay, I'll serve you one more. But it's the last one."

    B. "Sorry, but I could lose my job if I serve you one more."

Answer: B

Hopefully it is clear that there is a right and wrong way to handle the situation. The first statement is an agreement to do something illegal. The second statement tells the person that you are being firm; you will not change your mind about stopping service.

APPLY YOUR KNOWLEDGE

Did They Handle It Correctly?

Directions: Watch each video scenario provided by the instructor. Then decide whether employees handled the situations correctly. Circle the correct answer.

Scenario	Description	Was the Situation Handled Correctly?
1.	Intoxicated guest bothers another guest.	Yes No
2.	Intoxicated guest is rude to the bartender.	Yes No
3.	Intoxicated "regular" has a ride home.	Yes No
4.	Intoxicated guest is "drowning his sorrows."	Yes No

For answers, see page 4-19.

Drinks Passed to Guests after Service Was Stopped

What should you do if someone passes a drink to an intoxicated guest who's been cut off? →

You may stop service to a guest only to find that the person is still getting drinks from companions. If this happens:

- Tell your manager and any coworkers who should know.
- Stop alcohol service to the group. When you do, quote the law, and remember the communication techniques that you just learned.
- Take away the alcohol.

Before you do anything, make sure you are following company policy as well as state and local laws.

Intoxicated Guests Attempting to Leave

Stopping service to a person is only half the battle. You also need to do your best to make sure the person gets home safely. This can be challenging, especially if the person drove there alone.

One thing you **CANNOT** do is use physical force to stop a person from driving. So what should you do instead?

Try to talk the person out of driving. When an intoxicated person intends to drive, try to convince them not to.

If the guest still plans to drive. Follow these steps if the guest resists your initial attempt to talk him or her out of driving:

What should you do if an intoxicated guest insists on driving? →

- Warn the guest that you will call the police.
- If the guest insists on driving, call the police. Provide this information:

  » Make and model of the vehicle

  » License plate number of the vehicle

  » Direction of travel

If the guest agrees not to drive. If you were able to talk the guest out of driving, help the guest get home safely. Follow these steps:

● Accept the guest's car keys if they are offered.

● Arrange for alternate transportation. This might include any of the following:

  » Asking a sober companion to drive.

  » Calling the guest's friend or relative.

  » Calling a cab or arranging for another mode of transportation.

Intoxicated Guests with Designated Drivers

Can you serve guests to intoxication if they have a designated driver? →

Sometimes your guests may tell you that they have a ride home with a designated driver. This is someone in a group who agrees to not drink alcohol so they can safely drive the others home. (Some establishments even have designated-driver programs that provide special incentives, such as free soft drinks. Check to see if your place has a program like this.)

Many people think they will be allowed to drink to intoxication if they have a designated driver. That's simply not true. You are **NEVER** allowed to serve someone to the point of intoxication. And you should not, because you are still liable.

Guests Who Arrive Intoxicated

Sometimes, a guest might arrive at your establishment intoxicated. If this happens, try to keep the guest from entering the establishment. Remember:

● You always have the right to refuse service.

● Follow your company policy and state and local law.

If it's not possible to keep an intoxicated person from entering, treat the guest like you would anyone else who has had too much:

● Do **NOT** serve them alcohol.

● Offer food and nonalcoholic beverages.

● Make sure the guest gets home safely.

● Make sure coworkers know about the situation.

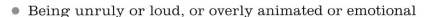

HANDLING POTENTIALLY VIOLENT SITUATIONS

What do you do when you think there's a potential for violence—or when things actually do become violent? The key is to anticipate problems.

Watch your guests. To anticipate a potentially violent situation, watch your guests. Look for these behaviors, which can quickly escalate into violence:

- Being unruly or loud, or overly animated or emotional
- Making inappropriate sexual or physical contact
- Arguing or making threats
- Throwing things, such as chairs or glasses

Be prepared. If it looks like a situation could become violent:

- Tell your manager and coworkers right away. They should be prepared and ready to help.
- Continue to watch the situation.

Put safety first. If anyone's safety is at immediate risk:

- Call the police. Do **NOT** wait for the situation to resolve itself. It usually won't.
- Try to keep bystanders out of harm's way.

Manage the situation. When it looks like a person will become violent:

- Stay calm.
- Ask the person to stop the behavior.
- Warn the person that you have called, or will call, the police.
- Do **NOT** get confrontational.
- **NEVER** touch or try to restrain someone you believe may become violent. Trying to touch or restrain someone puts your safety at risk. And it could have legal consequences.

HANDLING ILLEGAL ACTIVITIES

Another difficult situation is dealing with illegal activities on the premises. These include:

- Gambling
- Prostitution and other lewd behavior
- Weapons
- Drugs

As you learned earlier, you have certain responsibilities if you notice these things. But what exactly should you do?

- Consider safety. Do **NOT** take any action until you first consider your safety and the safety of your guests.
- Tell your manager. It's the manager's job to decide what to do.
- Call the police if required. Your manager may make this decision.

What should you do if you see a guest carrying a gun? →

Illegal Weapons

Some situations require extreme caution. For example, say a guest is carrying an illegal weapon. Unfortunately, you cannot just ignore this. In some states, an establishment can lose its liquor license if employees knowingly allow a person to have an illegal firearm on the premises.

If you see a guest carrying an illegal weapon:

- Do **NOT** confront the guest.
- Tell your manager.
- Follow company policy and state and local law. That may include calling the police.

Requests for Illegal Activities

You should always involve a manager when handling the situations discussed in this chapter so far. But what if someone asks you to do something illegal?

Requests from Management

What if your manager disagrees with a decision you made and asks you to respond differently? For example, your manager might ask you to continue serving a guest who you think is intoxicated.

If this happens, remember that you are liable for your actions while serving alcohol. Beyond this, you must always follow the law. If you think your manager is asking you to do something illegal:

- Express your concern.
- Respectfully decline.
- Contact the next level of management or your human resources department.

Requests from Coworkers

What if a coworker asks you to do something illegal, like serving underage guests or continuing to serve intoxicated guests? First, say no. Then tell your manager. While this may be uncomfortable for you, your coworker should not have put you in that position.

Requests from Guests

If a guest has made an illegal request or offered a bribe to continue service, do the following:

- Respectfully decline.
- Tell your manager.
- Communicate the situation to coworkers.
- Follow state and local laws and company policies.

DOCUMENTING INCIDENTS

When certain incidents occur, such as stopping alcohol service, your establishment may require you to complete an incident report. This is a written record of an event. These are used for two reasons:

- To help the owners and operators prepare for possible legal action
- To help determine if alcohol service policies are effective

Incident reports are not usually required by law. If you own or manage an establishment and you are trying to decide whether to use incident reports, seek legal advice.

If you work at a place that uses incident reports, follow your company policy on when and how to record an incident.

HANDLING FAKE OR ALTERED IDs

Dealing with a guest who gave you a fake or altered ID can be tricky. When handling these situations, always be polite and use the good communication techniques you've learned in this chapter. Whatever you do, avoid being judgmental or rude. And make sure you always tell managers and coworkers what happened.

APPLY YOUR KNOWLEDGE

From the Trenches

Directions: Listen to each person's story and then decide if he or she acted correctly by circling Yes or No.

	Scenario	Description	Was the Situation Handled Correctly?
1.		"Last night, a young couple came in all dressed up and ordered a bottle of champagne with dinner. When I asked for ID, the guy had an expired license that might have been his brother's, and the girl's looked like someone had doctored the photo.	**Yes**
		So I said, 'I'm really sorry, but it's against the law for me to accept these IDs.' Then I suggested some sparking water or nonalcoholic cocktail instead. They were disappointed, but they got over it. I made sure to let my manager and everyone else know what was going on."	**No**
2.		"Weekends are crazy here. When I went to use the restroom last Saturday, a couple of women were crammed into one of the stalls, giggling and snorting. Then they came out. One wiped away some white powder that was under her nose.	**Yes**
		How could I ignore that? So I told my friend who was their server that they were using drugs. But she said they'd just asked for the check and were leaving anyway, so we didn't need to do anything about it. Honestly, I was kind of glad."	**No**

4-16 ServSafe Alcohol Guide

	Scenario	Description	Was the Situation Handled Correctly?
3.		"So a guy came in and sat down at the end of the bar next to another guy. Things seemed fine. Then all of the sudden, they started arguing and shoving each other. So I called the police. Then I got my manager. Together we got the other guests out of the way then tried to calm down the two guys. We didn't try to separate them. No way I was getting in the middle of that! But I made sure they knew I'd called the police. That seemed to get their attention, and they backed away from each other. That was just about the time the police arrived. Not gonna lie, it was pretty scary."	**Yes** **No**
4.		"You're gonna love this one. Other afternoon a bunch of guys came in, ordered a couple pitchers of beer, sat at the farthest table, and started playing cards. No big deal, right? But when I went over to see how they were doing, they had a full-blown poker tournament going on! You wouldn't have believed how much cash was on the table. So I told my manager, and he called the police. Crazy, right?"	**Yes** **No**
5.		"These three young guys came to watch the game, and all of their IDs were suspicious. Probably fakes, So I said, 'You think you're so smart with these fakes? Sorry guys, no way! Come back when you're adults.' Their faces got so red! I told my manager I refused the service, and some of my coworkers thought it was hilarious when I told them what I said."	**Yes** **No**
6.		"It was another busy Saturday night. And as usual, I'm at the door carding people. A couple kids wanted in. One was old enough, but the other gave me a fake. And it's policy to confiscate fake IDs. So I broke the bad news to her. I said, 'Sorry, I can't let you in. And unfortunately, the law says I have to take your ID, too'. She was mad, but didn't argue. Afterward, I told my manager and coworkers what happened."	**Yes** **No**

For answers, see page 4-19.

VISITS FROM THE LIQUOR AUTHORITY AND LAW ENFORCEMENT

What should you do when law enforcement or the liquor authority show up? →

To make sure your establishment is following liquor laws, liquor authority agents and law enforcement officials can show up at any time. They do not have to tell you when they are coming. While these visits may be routine, they can still feel stressful.

When someone from the liquor authority or law enforcement visits your establishment:

- Politely ask for identification.

- Tell your manager and coworkers.

- Follow any related company policies.

You have the right to ask officials why they are there. You also have the right to ask them questions if you need to clarify what they are saying to you. Taking notes is also a good idea.

SELF-CHECK

Directions: Read the question and choose the best answer.

1. **When stopping service, which statement should you avoid?**
   A. "You've had enough."
   B. "I want to make sure you get home safely."
   C. "It's against the law for me to serve you any more alcohol."
   D. "Company policy does not allow me to serve you any more alcohol."

2. **What is one thing you should do if a fight happens?**
   A. Contact the liquor authority.
   B. Wait to see if it ends on its own.
   C. Move other guests away from the fight.
   D. Separate the people by pushing them away from each other.

3. **To prevent an intoxicated person from driving, you should**
   A. have the person's car towed.
   B. block the person from leaving.
   C. confiscate the person's driver's license.
   D. warn the person that you will call the police.

4. **When stopping alcohol service, you should**
   A. ask the person's companion to help.
   B. warn the person that you will call the police.
   C. count the drinks consumed and check a BAC chart.
   D. have your back-up next to you when you tell the person.

5. **When is the best time to tell a person that you have to stop alcohol service?**
   A. Before the person has ordered food
   B. As you serve the person's last drink
   C. When the person wants to order another drink
   D. After you have arranged a safe ride home for the person

6. **Which statement is true?**
   A. Serving intoxicated people is legal if they are not driving.
   B. Designated drivers are responsible for how much their people drink.
   C. Serving intoxicated people is illegal even if they have a designated driver.
   D. Establishments are not liable for intoxicated guests if the guests have a designated driver.

7. **Which should you avoid when telling people that you have to stop service?**
   A. Being firm
   B. Using "you" statements
   C. Expressing genuine concern
   D. Telling them you understand

8. **You see a drug sale on the premises. What should you do?**
   A. Tell your manager.
   B. Ask the people to leave.
   C. Watch for violent behavior.
   D. Tell the people that their behavior is illegal.

For answers, see page 4-20.

Answer Key

Apply Your Knowledge: Did They Handle It Correctly?

1. **No**, the bartenders did not handle the situation correctly. While the first bartender got a back up, her back up stood too close to the guest. This can be threatening. And while she waited until the guest ordered the next drink to stop service, the way she told him was judgmental. Moreover, neither of the bartenders offered the guest food or nonalcoholic beverages as an alternative.

2. **No**, the bartender did not handle the situation correctly. The bartender was initially polite when stopping service and offered nonalcoholic beverages. But the situation went downhill quickly. He ended up losing his temper and using judgmental language.

3. **Yes**, the bartender handled the situation correctly. First, she alerted a backup before stopping service. She also asked her coworker to let everyone know what she was doing. Then she waited until the guest ordered his next round before speaking up. When the guest kept trying to get a drink, the bartender held her ground. And she offered him food and other nonalcoholic alternatives.

4. **Yes,** the bartender handled the situation correctly. She told another server to alert the manager for backup and to tell their coworkers about the situation. Then she diffused the situation by not being judgmental and by being empathetic. She also offered food and nonalcoholic beverages. And most importantly, she called a relative to come and pick up the man.

Apply Your Knowledge: From the Trenches

1. **Yes**, the server handled the situation correctly. She expressed empathy and explained why she could not accept the IDs by citing the law. She also made sure her manager and coworkers knew the situation.

2. **No**, she did not handle the situation correctly. A problem does not go away because a guest leaves or it looks like they are leaving. Instead of just ignoring it, she should have told her manager and followed her company's policy and state and local laws.

3. **Yes**, she handled the situation correctly. It is okay that she called the police before telling her manager because her guests were in immediate danger. Then she and the manager tried to keep things calm, and they moved other guests out of the way.

4. **Yes**, he handled the situation correctly. When he saw the illegal gambling, he told his manager, and they followed company policy and state and local law.

5. **No**, she didn't handle the situation correctly. She was judgmental and rude.

6. **Yes**, the door person handled the situation correctly. Not only did he use good communication techniques to tell her, but he was also polite and remembered to tell his manager and coworkers about the situation.

Self-Check

1. A

2. C

3. D

4. A

5. C

6. C

7. B

8. A

Notes

INDEX

Notes

Notes

Notes

Notes

Notes

Notes